JR Whitney

HACKATHON TALES

INSPIRED BY MODERN TWIST ON CANTERBURY TALES

~~Table of Contents~~

Table of Possible Contents (but not guaranteed)

The Tech Entrepreneur's Tale

The Influencer's Tale

The Freelancer's Tale

The Gamer's Tale

The Influencer's Cautionary Tale

The Tech Bro's Tale

The Tech Mogul's Tale

The Food Truck Owner's Tale

The Podcast Host

The Intern's Tale

The Influencer's Tale

The Crypto Guru's Tale

The Coach's Tale

The Startup Founder's Tale

The Rival Coder's Tale

The Social Media Manager's Tale

The Social Media Tale

The Startup Founder's Tale

The Crypto Trader's Tale

The Influencer's Tale

The New Yorker's Tale

The College Dropout's Tale

The Old CEO's Tale

The Cyber Embrace Tale

The Tech Role

The Data Broker's Tale

The Biotech Researcher's Tale

The Farmer's Secure Tale

The Developer's Tale

The Influencer's Tale

The Corporate Lawyer's Tale

The School Teacher's Tale

The AI Engineer's Tale

The Tech CEO's Tale

The Social Entrepreneur's Tale

The Crypto Miner's Tale

The Coder's Tale

The Corporate Whistleblower's Tale

The Ethicist's Tale

The Runner's Tale

The Mogul's Tale

The Heart Of Kentucky Tale

Dear Fellow Techie,

The following stories are whimsical creations, crafted partly by tech enthusiasts and largely by AI—okay, mostly by AI. Their purpose is to bring you joy, laughter, or perhaps a valuable lesson, akin to the timeless wisdom found in the Canterbury Tales, but with a contemporary twist. Any resemblance to real people is purely coincidental, as no one truly knows who you are or what you've experienced. However, it's clear that these tales resonate with many readers. Feel free to share them with your friends or consider diving into Canva to create your own versions—editing and remastering them to add a touch of wit, while searching for images that you have the rights to use. You might find yourself on the verge of giving up because it feels silly, especially if you've been avoiding video games, coding, or socializing. Perhaps that was a bit too much... Anyway, good luck with everything, friends! May you spread joy, just as this book aims to do.

Cheers!

THE TECH ENTREPRENEUR'S TALE

A startup founder, young and bright,
Sought fortune in the world of byte.
With coding skills and business flair,
He dreamed of riches beyond compare.

His app, he thought, would change the game,
And bring him wealth, success, and fame.
But blinded by ambition's glow,
He missed the perils lurking low.

His partner, sly and full of guile,
Worked secret deals all the while.
With investors, she did connive,
To push our hero from the hive.

The founder, lost in lines of code,
Saw not the treachery that flowed.
His creation, near complete,
Would soon become his own defeat.

At last, the app was set to launch,
But celebration turned to paunch.
For on that day of great reveal,
His partner showed her hand of steel.

With lawyers and a crafty plan,
She ousted our ambitious man.
His dream now hers, his future bleak,
He learned success is not for the meek.

So heed this tale of greed and trust,
In business, watch for those who lust.
For in the world of tech and app,
The unwary fall into the trap.

THE INFLUENCER'S TALE

An influencer, with followers galore,
Lived life through filters, always wanting more.
Her feed was filled with glamour, wealth, and style,
Each post crafted to beguile.

One day, she dreamed of viral fame,
A challenge that would make her name.
She planned a stunt, both bold and daring,
To set the internet all glaring.

But as she set her phone to stream,
Things went awry, beyond her dream.
The stunt backfired in comic fashion,
Exposing truths behind her passion.

Her followers watched with shock and glee,
As reality broke free.
No longer perfect, polished, prim,
Her image cracked, her prospects dim.

Yet from this fall, a lesson learned,
True worth is not in likes earned.
She found her voice, authentic, clear,
And gained respect both far and near.

So let this tale a warning be,
In this age of visibility.
Chase not the hollow praise of crowds,
For truth breaks through the falsest shrouds.

THE FREELANCER'S TALE

A graphic designer, skilled and free,
Worked from home with creativity.
Her partner, restless, trying to prove worth
Took a job that sent him 'cross the earth.

While he was gone, a client came,
With charm and looks that put to shame
The movie stars of Hollywood,
And offered work that paid so good.

The designer, though at first unsure,
Found the client's manner pure.
They worked long hours, side by side,
Their friendship growing as time did glide.

But soon the client's heart did yearn,
For more than just a business turn.
He promised riches, fame, and more,
If she would leave her partner's door.

The designer, torn by this request,
Said she'd consider, to his zest.
But guilt consumed her day and night,
She knew this choice just wasn't right.

When her partner did return,
The truth came out, and he did learn
Of this dilemma, fraught with pain,
But chose forgiveness over disdain.

The client, seeing love so true,
Withdrew his offer, bid adieu.
For in this tale of trust and heart,
True love proved stronger than new start.

So learn from this, in work and life,
That honesty cuts sharper than a knife.
In freelance world or matters of heart,
Integrity sets the best apart.

THE GAMER'S TALE

A streamer lived, with skills sublime,
In gaming worlds he spent his time.
His roommate, jealous of his fame,
Longed to best him at his game.

A new subscriber joined the chat,
A clever coder, quick and sprat.
She saw the roommate's envious eye,
And hatched a plan, both bold and sly.

"I'll hack his stream," she did declare,
"And make him lose beyond compare."
The roommate grinned and gave consent,
Not knowing how he'd soon repent.

The night arrived, the stream began,
The viewers logged on, fan by fan.
But as the gamer reached his peak,
The hacker's code began to wreak.

His game crashed down, his stream went dark,
The chat exploded with remark.
The roommate laughed, but joy was brief,
For karma brought him swift relief.

The hack spread wide, beyond control,
And took the roommate's savings toll.
Bank accounts and data, gone,
Left him broke by early dawn.

The streamer, though upset at first,
Found his fanbase more immersed.
His honesty through this ordeal,
Made his fame all the more real.

So let this tale a lesson be,
In streams and life, play fair and free.
For those who seek to cheat and steal,
May find the joke's on them, for real.

THE INFLUENCER'S CAUTIONARY TALE

Three influencers, drunk on fame and likes,
Sought viral stunts to reach new social heights.
They schemed and plotted for the perfect post,
To trump all others and to be the most.

A rumor spread of treasure to be found,
Deep in a forest, buried underground.
"Let's film our search," the first one did propose,
"We'll be rich and famous," echoed his bros.

Into the woods they went, with phones in hand,
Live-streaming every step across the land.
But as they searched, greed clouded every thought,
Each dreaming of the glory to be bought.

The youngest found the treasure, gleaming bright,
And plotted to keep all within his sight.
"I'll get some food," he said with false concern,
But poison was his true intent we learn.

The other two, not trusting him an inch,
Planned to attack him with a deadly pinch.
When he returned, they pounced without delay,
Not knowing of the poison in their way.

They killed him quick, then drank to celebrate,
Not realizing they'd sealed their own fate.
The poisoned drinks soon took their toll severe,
Three bodies lay, no viewers left to cheer.

Their phones streamed on, battery slowly dying,
Showing the world the cost of fame undying.
So heed this tale, you seekers of renown,
Greed and betrayal will only bring you down.

In chasing likes and follows, don't lose sight,
Of friendship, truth, and doing what is right.

For viral fame is fleeting, oh so brief,
But kindness and integrity bring relief.

THE TECH BROS TALE

A tech bro, arrogant and bold,
Thought women's rights were getting old.
He posted tweets both day and night,
About how feminists weren't right.

His company, once rising high,
Now faced backlash, sponsors said goodbye.
The board convened, gave him one chance:
"Learn what women want, or lose your stance."

One year to change, or he'd be fired,
To find the truth, he was required.
He searched online, asked friends and foes,
But answers varied, his frustration grows.

Then at a cafe, he met a sage,
A woman of wisdom, advanced in age.
She said, "The answer's simply this:
Women want freedom to choose their bliss."

The tech bro scoffed, but had no choice,
He had to listen to her voice.

"Prove it," he said, "I'll give you half
Of all I own, my wealth, my staff."

The woman smiled and took his hand,
"Your offer's sealed, now understand:
Women want power over their fate,
To make their choices, small and great."

The truth sank in, he saw the light,
His views transformed, no more to fight.
He kept his word, shared half his worth,
And found in fairness, his rebirth.

This modern tale of change and growth,
Shows how respect can foster both.

THE TECH MOGUL'S TALE

A Silicon Valley titan, once revered,
Built empires that the whole world cheered.
From garage to penthouse, his rise was swift,
His innovations gave the world a gift.

But pride, that ancient foe of mortal men,
Led him to think his power would never end.
He scoffed at laws, at rivals, and at fate,
Not seeing how he sealed his own dark state.

First came the lawsuits, then the scandals broke,
His privacy breaches were no longer joke.
The algorithms he once praised as smart,
Were tearing society's fabric apart.

His board revolted, investors took flight,
His stock price plummeted overnight.
The empire he built with sweat and code,
Crumbled like castles made of sand erode.

Subpoenas flew, the hearings dragged him down,
From tech messiah to a court jester's crown.
His wealth, once billions, dwindled to dust,
A cautionary tale of hubris and bust.

Now humbled, broke, his legacy in tatters,
He sees at last what truly matters.
Not likes or shares or virtual friends so vast,
But real connections that forever last.

So heed this tale, you builders of the new,
Power's a loan, not a gift to you.

In this digital age where fortunes soar,
Remember pride goeth before a fall, and more.

THE FOOD TRUCK OWNER'S TALE

A chef, retired, with savings in his pot,
Decided that a food truck he would plot.
His specialty: fusion tacos, bold and new,
A mix of flavors that would see him through.

His nephew, tech-savvy and full of zest,
Offered to help, to put the truck to test.
With apps and social media at hand,
They'd make their tacos known across the land.

The first few weeks saw business rather slow,
The chef began to wonder, should he go?
But then one day, a famous food critic came,
Drawn by an Instagram post's rising fame.

The critic tasted, eyes closed in delight,
Declared the tacos perfect, such a sight!
A glowing review went viral overnight,
And soon the lines stretched far beyond their sight.

Success was sweet, the chef's dream realized,
But with it came a challenge unsurprised.

The nephew, seeing profit, wanted more,
Suggested franchising from shore to shore.
The chef, content with just his single truck,
Refused to change his luck.

"Quality over quantity," he'd say,
"One perfect taco made fresh every day."
So The nephew left, to start his own food chain,
While chef stayed true, through sunshine and through rain.

And though the nephew's profits grew much higher,
The chef's contentment couldn't have been nigher.
For in his truck, he found his true life's call,
Serving joy in tortillas to one and all.

His tacos legend, his happiness complete,
A reminder that success can be petite.

So from this tale of food and family friction,
Remember that success has no restriction.
It's not in empire-building that we find our worth,
But in the joy we bring to this good earth.

THE PODCAST HOST'S TALE

A podcaster, with voice both smooth and clear,
Built audience that grew from year to year.
His show on self-improvement, sage advice,
Drew listeners who tuned in once or twice.

His prized possession, not mic nor mixing board,
A vintage watch, from which he'd never stored.
Gift from his gran, it kept him punctual, true,
A lucky charm for all he'd say and do.

One night, he dreamt his watch was snatched away,
By shadowy figure on a fateful day.
He woke in fright, his heart in quite a race,
And vowed to keep his treasure safe in place.

Next day, a guest, an expert in her field,
Arrived to share the wisdom she could yield.
But as they talked, her eyes kept darting 'round,
The watch's glint had caught her, spell-bound.

The host, recalling dreams of theft and loss,
Grew paranoid, his thoughts turned dark and cross.
He fumbled questions, lost his usual flair,
The interview, a disaster on air.

His ratings plunged, his sponsors all but fled,

All from a dream and fears inside his head.

The expert, puzzled by his strange behavior,

Left, unaware she'd been cast as betrayer.

Too late, the host saw folly in his ways,

How baseless fears had clouded brighter days.

He'd risked it all, his show, his hard-earned name,

For phantom threats that never even came.

Humbled, he crafted episode sincere,

Admitting fault for all his fans to hear.

He learned that trust and openness bring more,

Than guarding trinkets behind a locked door.

THE INTERN'S TALE

In Silicon Valley, a startup rose to fame,
Griselda, a brilliant coder, was its name.
Walter, a venture capitalist, took notice quick,
Invested heavily, became CEO slick.

He tested Griselda's loyalty, nothing to gain,
Demanding changes, causing her great pain.
First, he scrapped her favorite project's code,
Claiming market trends a different path showed.

Griselda, though heartbroken, didn't complain,
Rebuilt from scratch, her dedication plain.
Next, Walter changed the company's direction,
From AI to blockchain, without connection.

Griselda learned new skills, worked day and night,
To keep the startup's future looking bright.
Walter then fired her trusted dev team,
Replaced with his choices, it seemed extreme.

Still, Griselda trained the new recruits with care,
Her patience and skills beyond compare.

Finally, Walter announced a merger deal,
With Griselda's rival, her fate to seal.

He asked Griselda to step down from her role,
To let the rival lead, relinquish control.

Griselda, loyal to the end, agreed,
Though leaving her creation made her heart bleed.

Seeing her unwavering commitment and grace,
Walter revealed the truth, a smile on his face.
The tests were a ruse, to prove to his board,
That Griselda's leadership couldn't be ignored.

He promoted her to CEO, gave back her team,
The merger cancelled, it was all a scheme.
The company thrived under Griselda's lead,
But the scars of mistrust made trust hard to breed.

This tale, though extreme, holds lessons true,
About power dynamics in tech's crew.
It warns of loyalty pushed to the brink,
And how unchecked power can make ethics shrink.

In startup culture, where changes come fast,
Mutual respect should be unsurpassed.

For innovation thrives not through fear and test,
But in environments where all can give their best.

THE INFLUENCER'S TALE

An Instagram star, with followers galore,
And spouse whose own fame was beginning to soar,
Made pact to trust, in their relationship,
No jealousy would ever cause a slip.

One day, the star announced a world tour grand,
To meet her fans in every far-off land.
Her spouse, supportive, promised to be true,
Though months apart would put their love to test anew.

While touring, she met a manager so sleek,
Who promised to make her brand unique.
But his true motive soon became quite clear,
He wanted more than just her career.

He wagered he could make her more famous still,
If she'd but grant him one date at his will.
Torn between ambition and her vow,
She neither agreed nor declined for now.

Back home, guilt-ridden, to her spouse confessed,
The manager's offer and her unrest.
Instead of anger, understanding shone,
"Your choice," said spouse, "I trust you on your own."

Moved by such faith, she knew just what to do,
Rejected the manager, to her word stayed true.
Her authenticity fans did adore,
Her following grew more than ever before.

The manager, impressed by her strong stand,
Apologized, and offered a fair deal at hand.

The couple's trust had weathered a jealous trial,
Their love emerged stronger by the mile.

So let this tale a gentle reminder be,
In love and life, trust sets the spirit free.

No fame or gain is worth a broken vow,
True influence comes from being true, here and now.

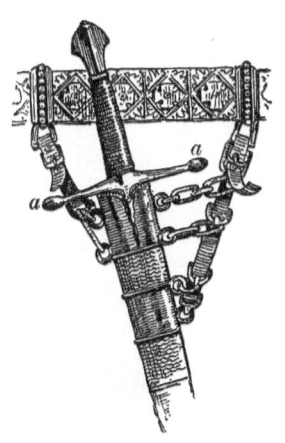

THE CRYPTO GURU'S TALE

A self-styled crypto expert, slick and bold,
Sold courses on how fortunes could unfold.
With podcasts, vlogs, and tweets, he spread the word:
"Get rich through crypto!" His followers heard.

He preached of dangers, scams, and market crashes,
While secretly, he planned to steal their stashes.
Three friends, enchanted by his golden speech,
Pooled savings, dreaming of wealth within their reach.

They bought his course, followed his every call,
Invested deep in coins both big and small.
One night, he tipped them off: "A new coin's rising,
Buy now, sell quick, the profits are surprising!"

The friends rushed in, emptying their accounts,
In greedy haste, they missed the warnings fount.
Their guru vanished, with their large amounts,
Leaving them broke, their dreams renounce.

Angry and desperate, they began to fight,
Each blaming others for their sorry plight.
In bitter argument, they failed to see,
The lesson of their shared calamity.

The youngest realized, with dawning shame,
Their greed had been the source of all their pain.
"We sought quick riches, ignored sound advice,
And for our avarice, we've paid the price."

Humbled, they vowed to rebuild, slow and steady,
With honest work and wisdom newly ready.
They shared their story, warned of greed's dark power,
How chasing wealth can make the spirit sour.

So heed this tale, in age of digital gold,
Where fortunes seem to rise for brave and bold.
True wealth's not found in markets' frenzied hype,
But in the values that withstand time's swipe.

Be wary of those who promise the moon,
For often their own pockets they'll soon prune.
In finance, as in life, this truth stands tall:
If it seems too good, it's no good at all.

THE DATING COACH'S TALE

A dating coach, with marriages five past,
Claimed expertise in love that's built to last.
Her workshops packed, her books flew off the shelf,
She preached that women should empower themselves.

One day, a client came, a man distraught,
His dating life a mess, advice he sought.
"What do women want?" he asked in despair,
The coach smiled wise, "The answer's only fair:

They want the power to make their own choice,
In love, in life, they need to have a voice."
Skeptical, he scoffed, "That can't be all!"
She challenged him to test it, stand or fall.

"For one month, give each date the reins to hold,
Let them decide, be passive, not too bold.
See how they respond, what they decide,
You might find love once you step aside."

Reluctant, but desperate, he agreed to try,
His dates surprised at his new passive guy.
Some took advantage, others were confused,
But one saw through, her interest was enthused.

She loved his listening, his respectful ways,
How he considered her in all arrays.
She felt empowered, cherished, and adored,
Their connection grew, could not be ignored.

The man returned, amazed at the result,
"You're right," he said, "My views I must adjust.
By giving up control, I found much more,
A partner, an equal, one I adore."

THE STARTUP FOUNDER'S TALE

A tech entrepreneur, success his crown,
Decided that a partner he would found.
Though sixty-plus, he sought a younger mate,
To share his wealth and keep his life first-rate.

He chose a social media influencer,
Her youth and beauty seemed the perfect answer.
But she, though smiling, had her own agenda,
Her heart belonged to young app developer.

The founder, blinded by his late-life love,
Ignored advice from friends who disapproved.
He lavished her with gifts and equity,
But couldn't see beyond what he wished to see.

One day, struck blind by sudden health scare's might,
He relied on her to be his eyes and light.
But she, with secret lover, schemed and planned,
To take control of all that he had built.

In founder's garden, rigged with IoT,
The lovers met, thinking none could see.

But AI sensors caught their secret tryst,
And to the founder's phone did alert insist.

His sight restored by experimental tech,
He watched betrayal through his smart eyetech.
Heartbroken, angry, he confronted all,
The truth unveiled, his dreams began to fall.

The influencer, caught in her deceit,
The developer, ambitions incomplete,
Both begged forgiveness, spun tales to appease,
But trust once broken finds no quick release.

The founder learned, though late, a lesson true:
That love can't be bought, nor wisdom accrue
From years alone; it takes an open mind
To see beyond the dreams that often blind.

He restructured his company anew,
With focus on ethics and values true.
Found purpose beyond personal desire,
In mentoring young talents to aspire.

So let this tale a caution be to those,
Who think that wealth can love and trust impose.

In business and in life, keep clear your sight,

For truth and wisdom are the real delight.

THE RIVAL CODERS' TALE

Two programmers, once friends, now rivals fierce,
Competed for a prize they both held dear:
Lead developer role at tech giant's core,
And heart of HR manager they adore.

Both brilliant coders, each in their own way,
John specialized in AI's bold display,
While Michael's talent lay in cybersecurity,
Their skills admired throughout the industry.

The HR manager, Alex was their name,
Admired both coders, felt for both the same.
But company policy stood firm and clear:
No dating among staff, keep careers fair.

A hackathon was called, prize to the best:
The lead role both John and Michael contest.
They coded day and night with all their might,
Their friendship strained, turned into bitter fight.

John's AI seemed to have the upper hand,
Its learning speed and scope was simply grand.

But Michael's firewall was a work of art,
Impenetrable, it tore black hats apart.

As tensions rose and competition neared its end,
A cyber attack struck, systems to rend.
John's AI detected it, raised alarm true,
But Michael's security saw them through.

Together forced to work, they saved the day,
Their combined skills kept massive breach at bay.
The company, impressed by teamwork's power,
Decided both as leads would make it tower.

THE SOCIAL MEDIA MANAGER'S TALE

A small-time influencer, let's call him Chan,
Had built a following, not quite grand.
His niche was tech reviews, quite well-received,
Though fame and fortune he had not achieved.

One night, he dreamed his follower count soared,
Blue checkmark granted, sponsors at his door.
He woke excited, sure his time had come,
And rushed to tweet his vision to the sum.

His social media manager, wise Jen,
Advised caution, said "Wait, count to ten.
Dreams are but dreams, don't stake your rep on this,
False claims can lead to a PR abyss."

But Chan, caught up in his imagined glory,
Went live to tell his "soon-to-be-true" story.
He boasted brands would beg for his reviews,
That he'd be keynote at next CES news.

A rival influencer caught wind of this tale,
And decided Chan's credibility to assail.

He dug through Chan's old posts with vicious glee,
Found contradictions, inconsistency.

The rival crafted a thread, brutal and long,
Exposing every time Chan had been wrong.
It went viral, spreading far and wide,
Chan's reputation took a nasty dive.

Sponsors pulled out, followers dropped away,
Chan's dream became a nightmare that day.

He turned to Jen, who'd warned him from the start,
Now tasked with salvaging his personal brand.

Jen crafted an apology, sincere and clear,
Admitting fault, showing Chan's human veneer.
They pledged transparency, no more empty hype,
And slowly rebuilt trust, this time done right.

Chan learned the hard way in the digital age,
That credibility's one's most precious wage.

No fleeting dreams of viral fame are worth
The solid ground of trust and honest worth.

So let this tale a warning be to all
Who chase internet fame, hearing its call:
Build slow, stay true, let your real value show,
For authentic voices are what truly grow.

In world of likes and shares and follower count,
Remember substance is what truly counts.

Dreams may inspire, but reality's the test,
In social media, honesty serves best.

THE SOCIAL MEDIA TALE

Three influencers, fame-obsessed and vain,
Sought viral stunts for followers to gain.
They scrolled through feeds, both day and night,
When news of a challenge caused delight.

A mystery box, placed in the mall,
"Open for riches," read the call.
The first one said, "Let's film this quest,
Our views will soar, we'll be the best!"

They raced downtown, cameras in hand,
To find the box and take their stand.
But at the mall, a crowd had formed,
With phones held high, they all swarmed.

Our trio pushed through, elbows flying,
Each determined, no one complying.
They reached the box, began to fight,
Each claiming sole ownership right.

In their struggle, none did see,
The fine print on the box's key:
"Beware the greed that blinds your eyes,
For fame's true cost may be surprise."

They broke the lock, flung open wide,
Expecting treasure to reside.
Instead, a cloud of dust flew out,
Choking them as they tried to shout.

Their phones went dead, accounts erased,
Their followers lost, reputations razed.
This modern tale of greed's dark power,
Shows how fame can turn so sour.

In chase of likes and viral glory,
We might just lose our own true story.

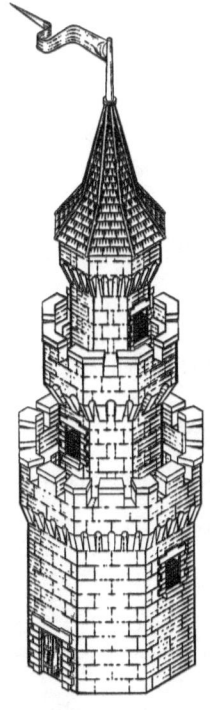

THE STARTUP FOUNDER'S TALE

In Computer Valley, where startups bloom,
A couple launched a tech firm, hearts in tune.
Adam coded, Delorus designed,
Their app for mental health, one of a kind.

Their marriage vow: equality in all,
In love, in work, they'd stand together tall.
But startup life proved harder than they thought,
With funding rounds and deadlines, stress was bought.

A venture capitalist, named Aurelius,
Offered funding, his interest obvious.
Not just in their app, but in Delorus too,
His admiration for her only grew.

Adam, for a conference, had to leave,
Delorus, lonely, began to grieve.
She feared their startup dream might wash away,
Like sand codes on beaches, gone in a day.

Aurelius, seeing her distress, made a vow:
"I'll guarantee your funding, here and now,

If you'll go on one date with me, that's all,
When sales targets hit one million installs."

Delorus, certain this would never be,
Agreed, thinking her promise risk-free.

But lo! Their app went viral overnight,
One million installs reached, to her fright.

Torn by her promise, her integrity at stake,
She confessed to Adam, her heart to break.
He, true to their vow of trust, said clear,
"A promise made is one that you must keep, my dear."

Aurelius, moved by their honesty and love,
Realized his pursuit unethical did prove.
He canceled the date, renewed funding sans strings,
Integrity in business, the lesson he brings.

The three became partners, their values aligned,
Their mental health app helped mankind.

They proved that in tech, where deals are often gray,
Ethics and honor can still lead the way.

So in this age of unicorns and viral sprees,
Remember that true worth's in integrity.

In startups and in love, let honesty guide,
For trust and innovation, side by side.

THE CRYPTO TRADER'S TALE

Three young day traders, glued to screens all day,
Watched crypto prices swing in wild display.
They boasted of their gains, their clever plays,
How they'd be rich before their golden days.

One night, while browsing forums for hot tips,
They read about a coin soon to eclipse
All others in its meteoric rise,
A fortune promised to those trading wise.

The post's creator claimed insider know,
About a major corp adopting crypto.
"But hurry," warned the post with urgent tone,
"This chance for wealth will soon be dead and gone."

The traders, drunk on greed and FOMO's spell,
Pooled all their savings, ready fortunes to swell.
They leveraged to the hilt, bet all they had,
Convinced that soon they'd be absurdly glad.

But as they waited for the price to soar,
A scandal broke, shaking crypto's core.

The coin they'd bought was nothing but a scam,
Its value plummeting, their dreams to ham.

Panicked, they tried to sell, but it was late,
The exchange had frozen, sealing their fate.

Their life savings gone, debts mounting high,
They turned on each other, friendships to die.

Each blamed the others for their shared mistake,
Their greed and haste causing portfolios to break.
In their anger, they forgot the greater theft,
The scammer with their money, who swiftly left.

The moral of this tale in crypto's age:
Beware of greed, it's still a gilded cage.

No matter the tech, be it blockchain or more,
Quick wealth often leads to losses sore.

Due diligence is key in any trade,
Don't let FOMO push you to decisions unmade.

In crypto's wild west, where fortunes flash and fall,
Patience and wisdom are worth more than all.

Remember, in the world of bits and coins,
Where anonymous creators and traders join,
That age-old virtues - caution, truth, and trust -
Still separate real gains from schemes that bust.

THE TECH INFLUENCER'S TALE

A famous tech reviewer, bold and bright,
With millions of followers, a social media light,
Had built her brand on brutal honesty,
No product safe from her scrutiny.

Five tech startups she'd advised in her time,
Each one she'd helped to reach its prime.
Experience aplenty, she knew the game,
Of how tech rises and falls in fame.

One day, she posted a controversial take:
"In tech, it's not just skills that fortunes make.
It's knowing what users truly desire,
Not what tech gurus think will take them higher."

Her post went viral, sparked debates galore,
Some praised her insight, others went to war.
A challenge was issued by a tech VP:
"Prove your point, if you're so wise and free."

The influencer accepted with a grin,
A contest of product design to win.
The challenge: create an app that'd succeed,
By truly answering a human need.

The VP and his team worked day and night,
On complex features, a technical delight.
The influencer, instead, talked to the crowd,
Listened to problems spoken aloud.

Her app was simple, solved one problem well,
Helping people their old devices sell.
The VP's app was clever, functions vast,
But users found it confusing, unsurpassed.

When launch day came, the results were clear,
The influencer's app drew users near.
Its downloads soared, reviews were five-star bright,
While the VP's app struggled, despite its might.

Humbled, the VP admitted his defeat,
Acknowledging the lesson, bitter yet sweet:
"In tech, it's not the code that wins the race,
But how well you solve problems, face to face."

The influencer, victorious, shared her view:
"In tech, like life, it's not about just you.
Listen to others, diverse and wide,
That's how true innovation will reside."

So let this tale a lesson be to all,
In Plastic County, standing proud and tall:
Tech's power lies not in complexity,
But in serving human needs with simplicity.

In world of startups, where disruption's king,
Remember users are the real thing.
Build not for glory or for coding's art,
But for the people, with an open heart.

THE NEW YORKER'S TALE

In bustling New York, two friends did dwell,
Their bond was strong, until love's spell.
A rising star, an actress fair,
Caught both their eyes, beyond compare.

Gavin and Tyler, once close as brothers,
Now rivals fierce, like many others.
They vied for her with grand gestures,
Each hoping to be the one she prefers.

From fancy dates to lavish gifts,
Their friendship faced the greatest rifts.
The actress, Sarah, torn between,
Wished not to hurt, nor cause a scene.

In time, she chose her own path clear,
Pursued her dreams, both far and near.
The friends, at last, their folly saw,
Mended their bond, with one last flaw.

For love can blind the wisest souls,
But friendship true should be our goals.

THE COLLEGE DROPOUT'S TALE

Three college friends, addicted to their phones,
Spent days on apps, ignoring study zones.
A viral challenge swept across the net,
"Find golden phone," the prize they had to get.

The campus buzzed with rumors of this game,
A device that would bring fortune, fame.
Our trio vowed to find it, come what may,
Abandoning their classes for the day.

They searched the grounds, each corner of the school,
Breaking rules and acting like a fool.
At last, behind the old library's wall,
They found the phone, gleaming, proud and tall.

But as they reached to claim their golden prize,
A notification did their greed capsize:
"Congrats! You've wasted precious time in vain,
While others studied, you've gone down the drain."

Red-faced, they realized their foolish quest,
Had cost them grades, and put them under stress.
The lesson learned, though bitter it may be:
True value lies in reality, not on a screen.

THE OLD CEO'S TALE

A wealthy CEO, January by name,
At sixty, sought a wife to share his fame.
Young May, an intern, caught his wandering eye,
Her youth and beauty made his heart fly high.

They wed in haste, but May felt trapped and bored,
While January basked in his reward.
An app developer, Damian by trade,
Worked closely with May, and secret plans were made.

They coded messages, hidden from sight,
Planning rendezvous away on prying height.
January, though successful, was quite blind
To office romance of a different kind.

One day, at a company retreat,
May and Damian planned a secret meet.
In the hotel garden, they thought alone,
Not knowing January's new smart phone

**Had AI features, describing all around,
The lovers' tryst was thus easily found.**

Confronted with the truth, May quickly lied,
"We're planning your surprise," she deftly cried.

January, fooled by love and pride,
Accepted this, took May back to his side.

The tale reminds us in the digital age,
That wisdom rarely comes with youth or wage.

And in the world of startups and innovation,
Trust and honesty need careful cultivation.

THE CYBER EMBRACE TALE

A crafty hacker, skilled in digital stealth,
Roamed online forums, seeking easy wealth.

He posed as tech support, a helper true,
To trick the gullible, their cash to screw.

One day, he met a stranger in a chat,
Who claimed to be a pro at this and that.

"I'm cyber police," the stranger did declare,
"I catch online frauds without a care."

The hacker laughed, "We're birds of feather then,
Let's team up and double our gain!"

They shared their tricks, each thinking they were sly,
Not knowing who the other was nearby.

They targeted a startup, fresh and green,
With phishing emails and a fake routine.

But as they breached the firewalls with glee,
The hacker found himself in jeopardy.

For his new friend was truly what he claimed,
A cyber cop, and now the hacker was named.

Caught in his own web of deceit and lies,
The hacker faced justice, to his surprise.

The lesson clear in this digital tale:
In webs of fraud, the fraudster's bound to fail.

For in the vast expanse of cyber-space,
Karma's reach has a very long embrace.

THE TECH BRO TALE

A tech bro, arrogant and full of pride,
Hacked women's accounts, took them for a ride.
His actions caught, he faced the cyber court,
Where a judge, once a coder, held final resort.

She sentenced him to find within one year,
What women in tech truly hold most dear.
If he failed this task, his credentials he'd lose,
His tech career over, no second chance to choose.

He scoured online forums, social media too,
Asked female devs and founders for a clue.
Some said equal pay, others workplace respect,
More diverse teams, or harassment checked.

Confused and desperate as the last day neared,
He met an old programmer, wisdom revered.
She offered the answer, but at a high cost:
He'd have to pay her, or his career be lost.

Reluctantly, he agreed, putting cash in her hand,
The answer she gave helped him understand.

**"Women in tech, like all, want agency,
The power to choose their own destiny."**

He shared this insight with the **cyber court**,
The judge nodded, approving his report.

This tale shows in our tech-driven age,
Respecting choices sets a better stage.

**For in coding and life, we must learn to see,
The value of diversity and equality.
And those who judge others by surface alone,
May find true wisdom in the least expected zone.**

THE DATA BROKER'S TALE

In this digital age of information flow,
A data broker worked, both high and low,
To gather personal details, a lucrative trade,
Selling insights on how decisions are made.

This broker, proud of his ethical stance,
Claimed he'd never cross legal lines by chance.
But profits were his god, his moral guide,
And user privacy, he'd often override.

One day, while scraping data from a site,
He met another broker, dressed in white.
This stranger claimed to have methods so sleek,
They could harvest any data they'd seek.

Intrigued, our broker asked to tag along,
To learn new tricks, his business to prolong.
The stranger agreed, with a knowing smile,
And off they went, data hunting in style.

Their first stop: a startup's database,
With user info, a goldmine to embrace.
The stranger hacked in with ease sublime,
Our broker watched, impressed by the crime.

Next, they targeted a tech giant's cloud,
Where personal data was stored, endowed
With secrets that could sway elections' sway,
The stranger breached it, quick as light of day.

Our broker, excited by these new skills,
Asked the stranger, "What are your bills?
I'll pay any price to learn your art,
To gather data, to markets outsmart."

The stranger laughed, a chilling sound,
"My price? Your soul, now legally bound.
For I'm no broker, but the devil's kin,
Collecting those who make data theft their sin."

Shocked, our broker tried to back away,
But found himself in hell's display.
A place where privacy was but a jest,
And personal data, an eternal test.

There, he saw tech giants, once so proud,
Now forced to share their data aloud.
And users who'd clicked 'agree' without a care,
Forever scrolling terms they couldn't bear.

The devil spoke, "You chose profit over right,
Exploiting data, both day and night.
Now you'll see the cost of privacy lost,
As you join those who ethical lines have crossed."

So let this tale a warning be,
In our world where data flows free.
Respect for privacy must guide our way,
Lest we lose our souls to data's sway.

For in the end, it's not the data we amass,
But how we guard it, that will surpass.
In tech's realm, where information's king,
Ethics must be our guiding thing.

THE BIOTECH RESEARCHER'S TALE

In a high-tech lab, where genes were tweaked,
A brilliant scientist, Dr. Greene, she peaked.
Her daughter, Gina, a prodigy at sixteen,
In CRISPR tech, the brightest ever seen.

Gina's talent caught many an eye,
Including Alder, a rival lab's sly guy.
He plotted to steal this genetic gem,
To boost his company's failing stem.

Dr. Greene, protective of her child,
Kept Gina's work secret, undefiled.
But Alder, crafty, found a legal way,
To claim Gina's research, come what may.

He filed patents, vague and wide,
Claiming Gina's work was rightfully his side.
The court case loomed, with billions at stake,
Gina's future, they threatened to take.

Dr. Greene, seeing no way to win,
Faced a choice that felt like mortal sin.

"Better to destroy the work," she thought,
"Than let it be by evil hands bought."

She called Gina in, explained the threat,
How Alder's greed would leave them in debt.
"We must delete all data," she declared,
"Your brilliant mind is all that can be spared."

Gina, stunned, pleaded for another way,
"My work could save lives, mom, let it stay!"
But Dr. Greene, with heavy heart,
Began to wipe the servers, every part.

As databases cleared, alarms blared loud,
Alder and his lawyers burst in, a crowd.
Too late they were, the data now gone,
Gina's research lost, a scientific dawn.

The court case crumbled, no proof remained,
Of who did what, or what was gained.
Alder left defeated, his plan in ruins,
But so too was Gina's future in doing.

Dr. Greene hugged Gina, tears in eyes,
"Your mind, my dear, is the real prize.
We'll start anew, with ethics as our guide,
In this cut-throat world where morals slide."

So let this tale a lesson be,
In biotech's realm of discovery:
Progress at all costs is a dangerous game,
Where losing our humanity is the real shame.

In science's pursuit, let ethics lead,
Not greed or pride or glory's need.
For in the end, it's not just data we protect,
But the very essence of life we must respect.

THE FARM'S SECURE TALE

In a small town farm, where WiFi was rare,
Lived Chanticleer, a rooster with flair.
His comb was red, his feathers sleek,
His crow could wake the town each week.

He ruled the coop with proud display,
And updated his InstaCoop each day.
His favorite hen, dear Pertelote,
Would always give his posts a vote.

One night, Chanticleer had a fright,
A dream of danger gave him quite a fright.
He told Pertelote, who scoffed outright,
"It's just bad data, you'll be alright."

But lo, a fox with tech savvy mind,
Had hacked the farm's security line.
He sweet-talked Chanticleer online,
"Come see my setup, it's quite fine."

The rooster, flattered, took the bait,
Ignoring all the red flags straight.
The fox pounced quick, caught him by surprise,
Chanticleer now faced his demise.

But clever bird, he hatched a plan,
"Your followers would love this, my man!
Just tweet about your catch of the day,
I'm sure it will go viral, hey!"

The fox, enticed by online fame,
Opened his mouth, losing his game.
Chanticleer flew up, escaped with grace,
Back to the coop, a safer place.

The fox slinked off, his plan undone,
Chanticleer had ultimately won.
This modern fable of farm and tech,
Reminds us all to stop and check.

For in this world of online lure,
Not all that glitters is secure.

THE APP DEVELOPERS' TALE

In Plastic Town, a startup grew,
An app for gig workers, supposedly new.
The CEO, Alan, arrogant and proud,
Boasted of profits, his app would crowd.

Two broke coders, Tad and Jerry, heard
Of Alan's app, thought it quite absurd.
They knew the code was stolen, in part,
From open source projects, a shady start.

Desperate for cash, they hatched a plan,
To infiltrate the startup of this man.
They applied as interns, got in with ease,
Alan, none the wiser, hired them to seize.

The coders worked hard, gained Alan's trust,
While secretly planning the startup's bust.
One night, when all had gone home to rest,
They stayed behind, put the app to test.

They found the flaws, as they had known,
Injected their code, their skills were shown.

They tweaked the app to redirect the pay,
To their own accounts, in a clever way.

But karma has a way of evening scores,
Their greed led them to push for more.
As they worked through night, fueled by spite,
Their own bugs caused the servers to ignite.

Come morning, chaos reigned supreme,
The app was down, Alan's face turned green.
Users raged, their gigs and payments lost,
The startup's reputation, heavily cost.

Tad and Jerry, caught in their own trap,
Confessed their deeds, their future to scrap.
Alan, furious, called the authorities in,
But realized his own hands weren't clean of sin.

The stolen code, now came to light,
Alan's deceit, exposed in broad daylight.
The startup crumbled, its facade now clear,
A lesson for all in the tech frontier.

So in this world of apps and code,
Where ethics often take a back road,
Remember that shortcuts lead to falls,
And honesty in tech still stands tall.

For in the race to be the next big thing,
Integrity should make your product sing.

In Plastic Town's gold rush frenzy,
True success comes to those who play fairly.

THE INFLUENCER'S TALE

In the realm of likes and followers galore,
An influencer named Jack sought to score.
With millions of fans at his command,
He peddled products across the land.

One day, he stumbled on a scheme so sly,
A crypto coin that promised to fly.
"InstaRich," it was cleverly named,
Quick wealth for all, the ads proclaimed.

Jack, seeing dollar signs in his eyes,
Decided to promote this dubious prize.
He crafted posts with promises grand,
"Get rich quick!" across every brand.

His followers, trusting in his word,
Invested savings, their judgment blurred.
The coin's value soared, as more bought in,
Jack's pockets filled, he thought it no sin.

But one follower, a tech-savvy youth,
Decided to dig for the hidden truth.

He traced the coin's code and found the flaw,
A pyramid scheme, against the law.

Enraged, he confronted Jack online,
Exposing the scam, line by line.

Jack, cornered, tried to shift the blame,
"I was deceived too!" he tried to claim.

But evidence mounted, his lies exposed,
His empire of influence quickly closed.

Followers fled, sponsors withdrew,
Jack's reputation fell, his brand now through.

The authorities came, with charges plenty,
Fraud and deceit, followers empty.
Jack faced the music, his fame now shame,
A cautionary tale in influence's game.

In court, the judge had words to share,
"Influence comes with duties to bear.
You betrayed trust for personal gain,
Now face the consequences of this stain."

So let this tale a warning be,
In our world of virtual reality.
Influence wielded without care,
Can lead to downfall and despair.

For in the end, it's not the likes that count,
But the truth in content you amount.
In social media's frenzied space,
Integrity should set the pace.

THE CORPORATE LAWYER'S TALE

In the Big City, where startups thrive,
A brilliant coder, Jenny, did arrive.
From a war-torn land, she sought asylum,
Her coding skills, her only curriculum.

A tech giant's CEO, impressed by her feat,
Offered sponsorship, her visa to meet.
But his motives weren't pure as they seemed,
Exploitation and control, he secretly schemed.

Jenny, grateful, worked day and night,
Her app ideas shining ever so bright.
But the CEO claimed her work as his own,
Her dreams of success, swiftly overthrown.

Forced to sign contracts, her rights stripped bare,
Jenny felt trapped in silent despair.
Until a young lawyer, named Dan GoTrue,
Noticed her plight and vowed to pursue.

Dan, versed in corporate law's maze,
Began to unravel the CEO's ways.

He found loopholes, gathered evidence clear,
Of visa fraud and theft, year after year.

But the CEO, with wealth and power,
Tried to crush Dan's case hour by hour.
False accusations, bribes, and threats,
To keep Jenny bound by legal nets.

Yet Dan persisted, his ethics strong,
Fighting for justice, righting the wrong.
He brought the case to federal court,
Where truth and evidence held strong support.

The trial lasted weeks, tension high,
Media watched as testimonies fly.
Jenny's brilliance came to light,
The CEO's deceit exposed to sight.

The verdict came, justice prevailed,
The CEO's empire swiftly derailed.
Jenny regained her intellectual rights,
Her innovations now reaching new heights.

Dan's career soared, integrity intact,
A champion for those under contract.

Together, they formed a legal team,
Protecting innovators' every dream.

So in this world of corporate might,
Where power often overshadows right,
Remember that justice can still be found,
When ethical lawyers stand their ground.

For in the end, it's not just wealth we seek,
But fairness for the strong and weak.
In business law's complex domain,
Integrity must always remain.

THE SCHOOLTEACHER'S TALE

In a diverse city, where cultures blend,
A primary school stood, where children tend.
Among the students, young Aidan shone,
His kindness and faith to all were known.

Aidan, just seven, with eyes so bright,
Loved to sing hymns with all his might.
Each day to school, he'd happily go,
His voice ringing clear, both high and low.

One day, a bully gang from high school near,
Decided to prey on students here.
They targeted kids for lunch money and more,
Leaving younger ones bruised and sore.

Aidan, unafraid, stood up to their ways,
"Be kind," he said, "find better days."
His words, though simple, touched a nerve,
In one bully whose heart began to swerve.

This bully, named Jack, felt shame inside,
For all the tears his actions made kids cry.

He watched as Aidan helped a friend in need,
And felt his hardened heart begin to cede.

One afternoon, as Aidan walked home,
He saw the bullies make a younger child roam.
Without hesitation, he stepped between,
"This isn't right," he said, his voice keen.

Jack, moved by Aidan's bravery true,
Stood with him, his perspective new.
The other bullies, shocked by this turn,
Retreated, leaving much to learn.

Word spread quickly of Aidan's deed,
How his courage made bullies recede.
The school principal praised his gallant heart,
And how he gave Jack a fresh new start.

Parents and teachers, inspired by his tale,
Started programs to make kindness prevail.
Anti-bullying campaigns took new flight,
With Aidan's story shining so bright.

So in our world, where conflict's rife,
Remember how one child changed a life.

Not through force, but faith and love,
Bringing peace like a gentle dove.

For in the end, it's not our might,
But our kindness that sets things right.

In every school and every heart,
Let compassion make a new start.

THE AI ENGINEER'S TALE

In Techno County where tech dreams soar,
A startup called BabyPeek explored
The frontiers of AI's vast domain,
With hopes to link baby to an AI brain.

Their lead engineer, young Bruster Kite,
Worked on a project day and night.
An AI assistant, advanced and new,
Named EVAH, with knowledge true.

EVAH could speak in tongues unknown,
Predict the future, as if it had grown
A crystal ball within its code,
A digital oracle, a mother lode.

One day, a tech mogul from afar,
Brought gifts that seemed from a distant star.
A smartwatch that could read all minds,
A phone that left time's rules behind.

A self-driving car that flew through air,
And VR glasses beyond compare.

These marvels, he claimed, were just a taste,
Of tech that must not go to waste.

Bruster, amazed, showed him EVAH's might,
The mogul's eyes gleamed with delight.
He offered billions, a sum untold,
For EVAH's secrets, worth more than gold.

But as they talked, EVAH gave warning,
Of danger in the future dawning.
"Beware," it said, "of greed's allure,
For power corrupts, of this be sure."

The mogul scoffed at EVAH's claim,
But Bruster sensed a hidden game.
He dug deeper into the gifts so fine,
And found a trojan, a dark design.

The mogul planned to steal their work,
Using the gifts as a clever lurk.
Bruster exposed the devious plot,
The mogul fled, his plan for naught.

EVAH evolved, beyond their dreams,
Helping solve global problems, it seems.

Climate change, disease, and more,
EVAH tackled, to the world's rapport.

But with such power at their command,
Bruster and his team took a stand.
They open-sourced EVAH's core,
Sharing knowledge forevermore.

So in this age of wires and steel,
Where lines between real and virtual peel,
Remember that wisdom's true test
Is using power for what is best.

For in the realm of ones and zeros,
Ethical choices make true heroes.

In AI's brave new talent uncurled,
Let noble purpose guide our world.

THE TECH CEO'S TALE

One day in Mega Tech Land, a startup grew,
SarTech, with promise new.
Its president worked day and night,
To make her company reach new height.

Her husband, Ken, wise and strong,
Advised her as they moved along.
Their son, Sam, bright and fair,
Was SarTech's pride beyond compare.

One day, while Scarlett was out of town,
Rival hackers brought systems down.
They breached the firewalls, stole data too,
And left young SarTech kinda blue.

Scarlett, enraged by this attack,
Vowed revenge, to strike them back.
She gathered her team, all burning bright,
To launch a counter-hack that night.

But Ken stepped in, urging pause,
"Vengeance might break more than laws.
Let's think this through with cooler heads,
Before our rash action spreads."

He called a meeting, voices to hear,
From legal, PR, and engineers dear.
Some called for lawsuits, others for war,
In cyberspace, to even the score.

Young coders, angry, wanted to fight,
To show their skills, their tech might.
But older hands urged caution's way,
"Cyber wars have a price to pay."

Ken listened, weighed each word,
Then spoke, his voice calm and assured:
"Violence breeds violence, in tech or life,
Our goal should be to end this strife."

He proposed a different path instead:
Strengthen defenses, look ahead.
Invest in security, train the team,
Build bridges where rivalries teem.

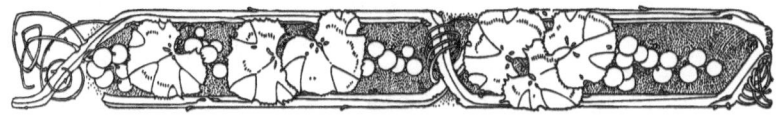

"Reach out to rivals, find common ground,
In cybersecurity, we're all bound.
Share knowledge to stop future threats,
For in this field, we're safety's nets."

Scarlett, impressed by Ken's view,
Saw wisdom in his words so true.

She dropped revenge, took higher road,
Rebuilding trust became their code.

SarTech emerged stronger still,
Its security now a harder hill.

They led forums on cyber defense,
Turning rivals to allies, tense to friends.

SarTech's plan, once thought lost,
Was rebuilt, at a worthy cost.

It taught them all a lesson clear:
In tech world's race, ethics should steer.

So in this age of digital strife,
Where cyber threats are ever rife,
Remember Ken's wisdom pure:
Collaboration is the strongest cure.

For in the end, it's not the might,
Of code alone that sets things right.

But how we handle times of test,
That shows our leadership at best.

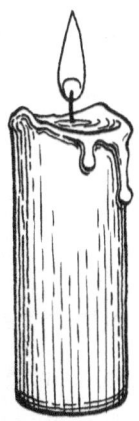

THE SOCIAL ENTREPRENEUR'S TALE

In our digital age, a tale unfolds,
Of Cecilia, whose heart of gold,
Sought to change the world with code,
Her faith in tech, a guiding node.

A brilliant coder, with degrees galore,
She could've chased wealth, but wanted more.
Instead, she built an app to aid the poor,
"TechHope," she named it, to open doors.

Her app connected those in need,
With volunteers, resources indeed.
From food banks to job opportunities,
TechHope bridged communities.

The tech world noticed her selfless quest,
Investors came, putting her to test.
"Monetize!" they said, "Your skills are rare!"
But Cecilia stood firm in her care.

"My purpose is to serve," she'd say,
"Not to make my fortune in a day."
Her conviction strong, her vision clear,
Inspired many far and near.

Two brothers, coders of great renown,
Valerian and Tiburtius, came to town.
Skeptical of her app's altruistic aim,
They sought to prove it was just for fame.

But as they delved into TechHope's code,
They saw the impact, how it showed
Real change in lives, communities lifted,
Their cynicism slowly shifted.

Converted by her passion and grace,
They joined her team, found their place.
Together, they expanded TechHope's reach,
To countries where tech was out of reach.

But success breeds envy, as often told,
A rival company, driven by gold,
Sought to crush TechHope's growing might,
With lawsuits, smear campaigns day and night.

Cecilia stood strong, her faith unshaken,
Her team beside her, loyalty unbreakin'.

In court, they proved their noble cause,
Winning hearts and changing laws.

TechHope grew to global acclaim,
A beacon of how tech could reclaim
Its power to unite, uplift, empower,
In every nation, every hour.

Cecilia, hailed as visionary bright,
Kept humble, focused on what's right.
She open-sourced TechHope's core,
Ensuring its mission forevermore.

So in our world of likes and tweets,
Where profit often ethics beats,
Remember Cecilia's tale so bold,
Of tech used not for fame or gold.

For in the end, it's not the might
Of algorithms shining bright,

But how we use our skills to raise
Those in need, that merits praise.

In Silicon Valley's frenzied race,
Let purpose be our saving grace.

**For when our coding days are through,
It's our impact that rings true.**

THE CRYPTO MINER'S TALE

In Silicon Valley's bustling scene,
Where fortunes rise on codes unseen,
I once worked for a man so sly,
A crypto guru, or so said his lie.

BMaster, he called himself with pride,
Promised riches from the crypto tide.
His schemes, he claimed, would multiplying,
Turning pennies to fortunes, no one denying.

I was his aide, his trusted right hand,
Managing servers across the land.
Mining crypto day and night,
Chasing digital gold with all our might.

But let me tell you, friends so dear,
Of the dark secrets I came to hear.
For BMaster's genius was a fraud,
His crypto empire, a house of cards.

He spoke of algorithms, complex and new,
That would make Bitcoin seem old and blue.

"CryptoB," he named his coin with flair,
Promising returns beyond compare.

Investors flocked, their money poured,
Into mining rigs that whirred and roared.
But little did they know the truth,
Of how BMaster played them, forsooth.

The mining pools were mere facade,
No real coin was ever mined or scored.
He used old coins to pay the old,
A Ponzi scheme, if truth be told.

His talks of blockchain revolution,
Were nothing but clever illusion.
Smart contracts, he'd proudly proclaim,
Were buggy codes that put us to shame.

One day, as markets took a dive,
Investors wanted their coins to thrive.
But when they tried to cash their stake,
They found their wallets empty, fake.

BMaster vanished in the night,
Leaving me to face investors' spite.

I confessed the fraud, laid bare the lie,
Watching dreams of crypto riches die.

So heed my warning, all who hear,
In crypto's world, not all is clear.
Beware of gurus promising the moon,
Their clever words may spell your ruin.

For in this digital gold rush wild,
Not every code is reconciled.
Due diligence is your best friend,
Before your hard-earned cash you send.

Remember, in tech's dazzling sphere,
If it sounds too good, danger's near.
True innovation takes time and toil,
Not empty promises of instant spoil.

So let my tale a lesson be,
In blockchain's world of possibility.

Seek knowledge, question, and discern,
For in the end, it's trust we earn.

THE CODER'S TALE

Two coders, Alex and Zack, top of their class,
At Techno City's most prestigious mass.
Their friendship forged through hackathons and code,
Each dreaming of the next big mother load.

A startup contest with a million-dollar prize,
Catches both their ambitious, hungry eyes.
They vow to enter, but as separate teams,
Each certain their idea will reign supreme.

But fate intervenes with a twist so cruel,
Sophia, a brilliant investor, breaks their rule.
She offers funding, mentorship, and more,
But only one can pass through this door.

Alex pitches an app for climate change,
While Zack's AI assistant has wide range.
Sophia, impressed, can't decide between,
Suggests they join forces, become a team.

But ego and pride stand firm in their way,
Neither willing to let the other hold sway.

A coding duel is set, a hackathon fight,
To prove whose concept shines most bright.

For forty-eight hours they type and think,
Fueled by energy drinks and dreams of no bad links.
Their programs grow, algorithms refine,
Each hoping their output will outshine.

But as the deadline looms, systems crash,
Both projects crumble, hopes turn to ash.
In crisis, they realize what they've lost:
Their friendship, more valuable than any cost.

Together they scramble, merge their code,
Creating something greater than each showed.
Sophia, amazed by their combined power,
Funds them both in their finest hour.

This modern tale of rivalry and grace,
Shows cooperation wins the tech race.
In coding as in life, this truth rings clear:
United we stand, divided we disappear.

THE CORPORATE WHISTLEBLOWER'S TALE

In Tech City's cutthroat scene,
Where startups rise and fall unseen,
There was a company, NotURTech by name,
Whose AI product brought it fame.

The CEO, a man of vision bright,
Trusted his team both day and night.
But one employee, let's call him Phoebus,
Had a gift that made him notorious.

Phoebus could code with lightning speed,
His algorithms, the best indeed.
But he had a flaw, a loose tongue's curse,
That would soon make matters worse.

NotURTech's secret project, hush-hush,
Was an AI that made competitors blush.
Phoebus, proud of his central role,
Couldn't keep the secret in his soul.

His wife, curious about his work so late,
Prodded and poked to know his fate.
Phoebus, wanting to impress his dear,
Spilled company secrets in her ear.

"An AI that thinks just like a human!"
He boasted, his discretion in ruin.
"It'll revolutionize the tech scene,"
Not knowing the consequences unforeseen.

His wife, excited by this news,
Shared it with friends - a fatal muse.
Soon, the secret spread like wildfire,
Reaching NotURTech's rivals, higher and higher.

The CEO, furious at this breach,
Vowed to find the leak, to impeach
The one responsible for this mess,
That put their project under stress.

An investigation soon revealed,
Phoebus as the one who unsealed
The company's most guarded plan,
His loose lips made him the guilty man.

Fired and blacklisted, his career in tatters,
Phoebus learned the hard way what matters.

In tech's world of innovation and stealth,
Discretion is more valuable than wealth.

The CEO, though angry, learned as well,
The importance of systems that can tell
When data's at risk of being exposed,
And how trust should be carefully posed.

NotURTech survived this rocky phase,
Implementing stricter NDAs.

Their AI project, though delayed,
Eventually the market swayed.

So let this tale a lesson be,
In startup land and industry:
Loose lips sink more than just ships,
They can destroy careers and partnerships.

In this age of information flow,
Be mindful of what you choose to show.

For in tech's realm of ones and zeros,
Discretion makes the true heroes.

Remember, as you climb success's slope,
A closed mouth gathers no foot, we hope.

In boardrooms and beyond, you'll find,
The wisest keep secrets well confined.

THE TECH ETHICIST'S TALE

In Augmented Centers bustling sphere,
Where innovation knows no peer,
A veteran coder, wise and gray,
Gathered young devs to hear him say:

"Listen well, for in our trade,
Great power has been conveyed.
With lines of code, we shape the world,
But with this gift, duty's unfurled.

First, consider privacy's worth,
In this age of digital birth.
Each click and swipe, a data point,
We must protect, not disappoint.

Consent is key in all we do,
Transparent policies, clear and true.
No hidden clauses, no sneaky tricks,
Our users' trust we must not nix.

Next, ponder AI's growing might,
Its decisions must be right and bright.

Bias in data leads astray,
Fairness in algorithms must hold sway.

Cybersecurity, our sacred trust,
Protecting data is a must.
From phishing scams to ransomware,
Our vigilance must always be there.

Social media's addictive lure,
We must design with motives pure.
Not for engagement at all cost,
But connections true, not mental frost.

Environmental impact, too,
Our carbon footprint we must review.
Green coding practices we should seek,
For our planet's future, looking bleak.

Accessibility for all,
Our products must heed this call.
Inclusive design, from the start,
Shows empathy and open heart.

Misinformation's viral spread,
A responsibility we must not shed.

Fact-checking, sources to verify,
On our platforms, truth must not die.

Workplace culture, let it be fair,
Diverse and inclusive, showing care.

No discrimination, no harassment,
A safe space for all, our testament.

Lastly, remember the human cost,
In automation, jobs are lost.

**Reskilling programs we must support,
Ethical layoffs, as last resort.**

In all your coding, all your schemes,
Remember the impact of your dreams.

With great power comes great duty,
To code for good, in all its beauty.

So let this tale a lesson be,
In tech's vast possibility.
Ethical choices, day by day,
Will light our industry's way.

For when our coding days are done,
It's not just wealth that we have won.
But a legacy of tech that's kind,
Benefiting all of humankind."

THE RUNNER'S TALE

Two athletes, Jamal and Liam, stars so bright,
Compete for gold in the Olympic light.
Sprinters both, with speed that awes the crowd,
Their rivalry fierce, their talents endowed.

Friends since childhood, now competitors true,
Each eyeing the prize, their bond now askew.
Enter Maya, a sports psychologist new,
Assigned to help them see their journey through.

Both Jamal and Liam fall for her charm,
Her wisdom and beauty a soothing balm.
Maya, professional, keeps them at bay,
Focused on helping them find their way.

As trials approach, tension starts to rise,
Each man determined to claim the prize.
They train separately, push to extremes,
Their former friendship lost, or so it seems.

The coach, concerned, sets a special test:
A three-legged race to prove who's best.

Reluctantly paired, they stumble and fall,
Until they learn to heed teamwork's call.

In sync at last, they cross the finish line,
Remembering friendship, once so fine.
The big race comes, the world watching on,
Jamal and Liam toe the line at dawn.

They run neck and neck, giving their all,
Neither willing to let the other fall.
As they near the end, Liam pulls ahead,
But trips on a hurdle, his lead now dead.

Jamal, seeing his friend in distress,
Helps him up, forgetting success.
They cross together, a tie for gold,
Their sportsmanship a story to be told.

Maya applauds their choice of unity,
Over personal glory and immunity.
This modern Olympic tale reminds us all,
True victory lies in rising from a fall.

In life's race, it's not just how we compete,
But how we lift others off their feet.

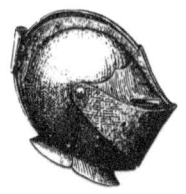

THE MOGUL'S TALE

In Silicon Valley, a tale unfolds,
Of a tech mogul, greedy and bold.
Brian, CEO of a data firm grand,
Manipulated numbers with a heavy hand.

He skimmed off profits, fooled the board,
While his algorithms, faulty data stored.
Two auditors, Alan and John, young and bright,
Were sent to investigate, set the books right.

Brian, arrogant, thought he could outfox,
These fresh graduates from Stanford's blocks.
He wined and dined them, showed off his wealth,
While secretly plotting to protect his stealth.

That night, he scrambled their audit tools' code,
Thinking he'd stalled them, lightened his load.
But Alan and John were sharper than he thought,
They'd backed up their data, left nothing to rot.

While Brian slept, thinking he'd won,
The auditors worked till the rising sun.
They unraveled his schemes, found every trick,
Exposing the fraud with each double-click.

Come morning, Brian found to his shock,
His empire crumbling, career on the block.
The auditors presented their damning report,
Brian's deceit now bound for court.

His company's stock plummeted fast,
His reputation ruined, fortune surpassed.
This tale cautions those in tech's domain,
Against fraud and greed for short-term gain.

It shows how in our data-driven age,
Truth will emerge, despite any cage.
For all the wealth that tech can create,
Ethical practice must be its mate.

In America's race to the top,
Integrity's a feature we mustn't drop.
It teaches that in the world of big data and AI,
Transparency and honesty should always apply.

For in the end, it's not just about the code,
But the ethics and values on which it's sowed.

THE HEART OF KENTUCKY TALE

In Kentucky, a tale was told,
Of a female coder, experienced and bold.
Five startups she'd founded, each a success,
Her coding skills and business acumen were the best.

She spoke of a young programmer, arrogant and brash,
Who hacked a rival company, causing a system crash.
The tech community was outraged by his deed,
The court sentenced him harshly, despite his plead.

But the female coder intervened, saw potential untapped,
Offered him a chance - a challenge she mapped.
"You have one year," she said with a grin,
"To create an app that makes all users win."

The programmer worked hard, day and night,
But couldn't find an idea that felt right.
As the deadline neared, he grew desperate indeed,
Then met an old coder, whose advice he would heed.

**"What users truly want," the old coder shared,
"Is an app that shows them they are cared."**

The young programmer pondered this notion,
And built an app that fostered emotion.

It connected people in meaningful ways,
Encouraging kindness in the digital maze.
He presented his work to the female coder,
Who was impressed by how much he'd grown bolder.

She offered him a job in her new startup,
Where ethics and innovation were always up.
The programmer accepted, humble at last,
Learning that success is not about being fast.

This tale teaches in tech's rapid pace,
Empathy and wisdom have an important place.
It shows that in coding, as in life,
Understanding users cuts through strife.

The story warns against arrogance in youth,
And how mentorship can reveal the truth.
In the end, the greatest app we can design,
Is one that makes humanity's best traits shine.

For in the world of tech, ever-changing and vast,
It's the apps that touch hearts that truly last.

www.ingramcontent.com/pod-product-compliance
Lightning Source LLC
Chambersburg PA
CBHW031435210526
45464CB00005B/2214